The Human Brain

Inside Your Body's Control Room

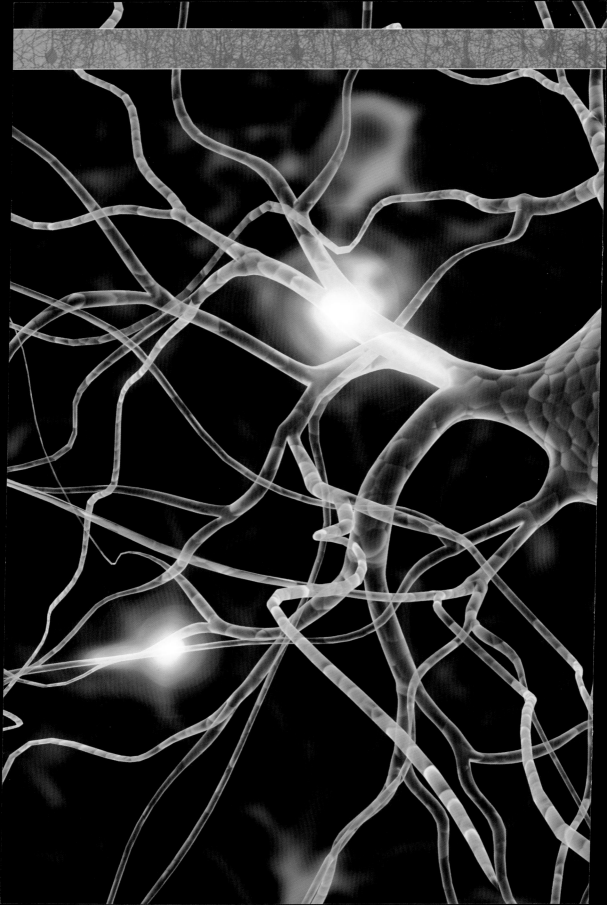

The Human Brain

Inside Your Body's Control Room

By Kathleen Simpson

Dr. Lori Jordan, Consultant

NATIONAL
GEOGRAPHIC

Washington, D.C.

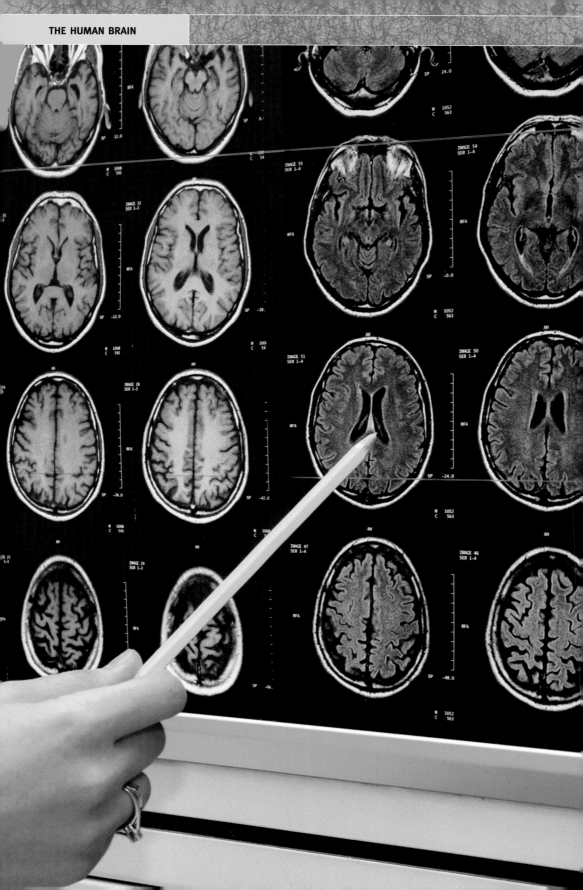

Contents

< Cross-sections of a brain as seen by magnetic resonance imaging (MRI).

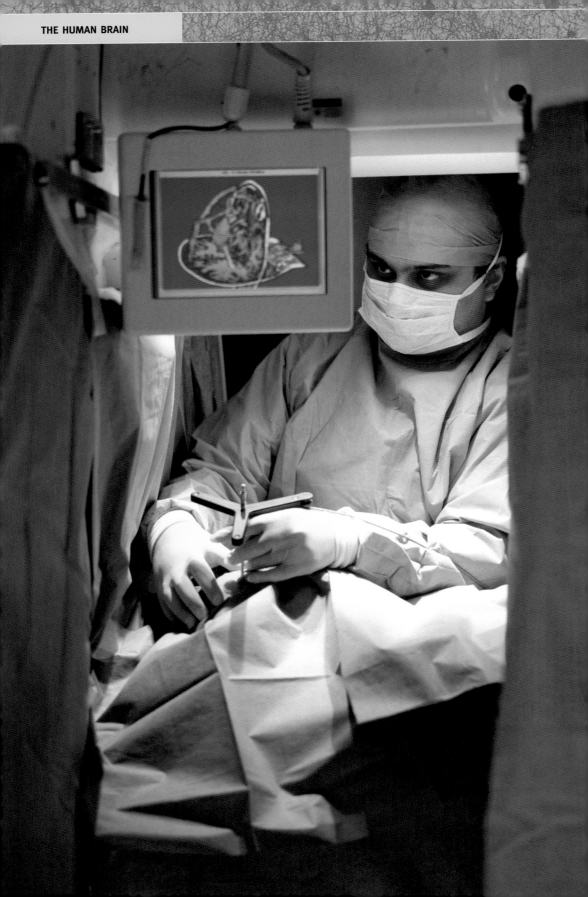

< A surgeon uses magnetic resonance imaging (MRI) to remove a brain tumor from a patient. The screen in the foreground highlights the location of the tumor (in green).

I n this book, you will learn about the anatomy of the brain and the basics of what we know about how the brain functions. This book will explain some things you've always wanted to know— What is memory? What happens when we sleep? But, you may also think of questions about the brain that aren't covered in this book. The brain is so complex that we still don't understand what all the areas of the brain do. What we know now is exciting and what we will learn in the future is even better. This book describes some of the fascinating ways that leading neuroscientists are studying the brain and our emotions.

The 1990s were called "The Decade of the Brain" because our country was focused on advancing brain research. Just because the 1990s have come and gone doesn't mean that our interest in the brain has lessened. There is so much to be gained from studying the brain. We will find new ways to treat people with neurological (brain) disorders, new ways to prevent injuries to the brain from happening, and will learn more about how we think and feel. Start with this book, and keep on learning.

What about your brain? Remember that your brain needs "exercise" just like the rest of your body. Push yourself to learn new things, especially those subjects that are hard for you—stretch your mind! Taking good care of yourself is good for your brain. Wearing a bike helmet to prevent injury and not smoking are just two things you can do to keep your brain healthy.

Lori Jordan
Baltimore, 2008

A Diagram of the Brain

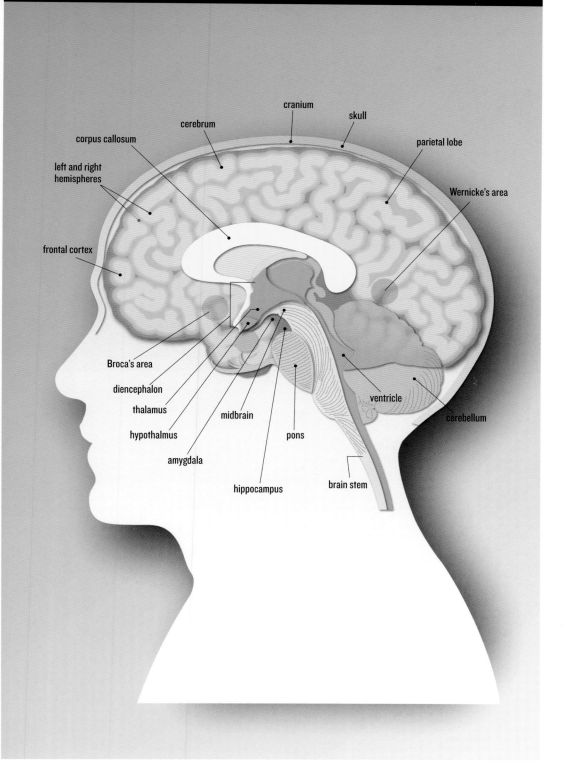

< **5000 B.C.** · A skull with a hole cut into the forehead indicates ancient medical practices included a form of brain surgery.

V **1700 B.C.** · The Edwin Smith Papyrus is the world's oldest surviving description of surgery.

Λ **1402** · A print from artist Will Hogarth depicts patients in a mental ward at St. Mary of Bethlehem Hospital in England.

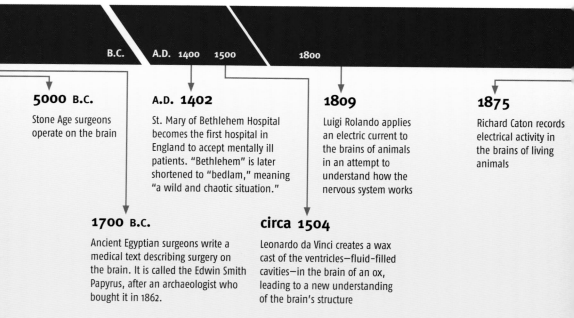

B.C. | A.D. 1400 | 1500 | 1800

5000 B.C.

Stone Age surgeons operate on the brain

A.D. 1402

St. Mary of Bethlehem Hospital becomes the first hospital in England to accept mentally ill patients. "Bethlehem" is later shortened to "bedlam," meaning "a wild and chaotic situation."

1809

Luigi Rolando applies an electric current to the brains of animals in an attempt to understand how the nervous system works

1875

Richard Caton records electrical activity in the brains of living animals

1700 B.C.

Ancient Egyptian surgeons write a medical text describing surgery on the brain. It is called the Edwin Smith Papyrus, after an archaeologist who bought it in 1862.

circa 1504

Leonardo da Vinci creates a wax cast of the ventricles—fluid-filled cavities—in the brain of an ox, leading to a new understanding of the brain's structure

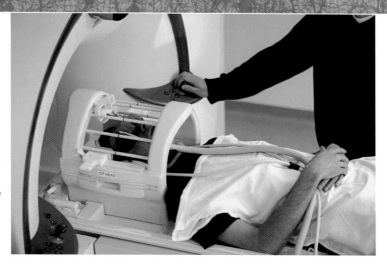

> **1992 · A patient receiving an fMRI (functional magnetic resonance imaging) wears special glasses to measure visual activity. Doctors will then study the areas of the brain affected as indicated on the fMRI.**

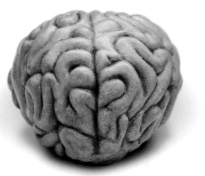

∧ **1954 · The human brain is divided down the middle into two distinct hemispheres, each controlling specific functions in the body.**

∧ **2004 · Dr. Linda Buck**

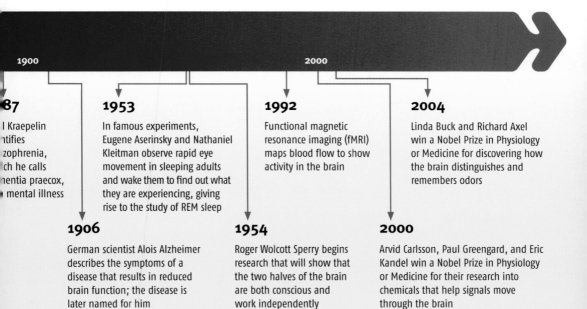

1900   2000

87

I Kraepelin
ntifies
zophrenia,
ch he calls
mentia praecox,
mental illness

1953

In famous experiments, Eugene Aserinsky and Nathaniel Kleitman observe rapid eye movement in sleeping adults and wake them to find out what they are experiencing, giving rise to the study of REM sleep

1992

Functional magnetic resonance imaging (fMRI) maps blood flow to show activity in the brain

2004

Linda Buck and Richard Axel win a Nobel Prize in Physiology or Medicine for discovering how the brain distinguishes and remembers odors

1906

German scientist Alois Alzheimer describes the symptoms of a disease that results in reduced brain function; the disease is later named for him

1954

Roger Wolcott Sperry begins research that will show that the two halves of the brain are both conscious and work independently

2000

Arvid Carlsson, Paul Greengard, and Eric Kandel win a Nobel Prize in Physiology or Medicine for their research into chemicals that help signals move through the brain

The Very Young Brain

CHAPTER 1

How Do We Learn?

Long before you came into this world, your brain began to take shape—a wet clump of cells containing no memory, no joy or anger, and no ideas about who or what you were. Each day, those cells divided, slowly growing into a well-developed, healthy brain. At birth, your brain was dull pink in color and weighed three quarters of a pound or a little more (350 to 400 g). It contained about 100 billion nerve cells, along with billions of other types of cells. Soft, wrinkly, and very delicate, it was the most powerful organ in your body. Because of your brain, you were able to feel, to wonder, and to learn.

In your first year of life, your brain almost tripled in size. It learned to make sense of the blurry images

< Studying the brains of newborns gives researchers insight into how we learn—and how learning changes the brain's structure.

your eyes sent it. It learned to recognize faces, and it found some more important than others. As an endless song of sounds played into it, your brain sorted through them and focused on voices and words.

Investigating Babies' Brains

Babies' brains work fast, gathering information, organizing it, coming up with theories about the world around them, testing those theories, and retesting them constantly. One of the most complex skills that babies learn is language, yet they seem to be better language learners than adults. Scientists would like to know more about how babies learn, but studying their brains is not easy. Because babies cannot speak or follow instructions, scientists must invent ways to investigate young brains.

In a famous experiment, a psychologist named Andrew Meltzoff leaned over a curious baby and stuck out his tongue. The baby hesitated a moment and then stuck out her tongue, too. Meltzoff's experiment, performed many times with babies as young as 42 minutes, showed that people are born knowing how to learn from others. Their brains are programmed with

∧ A baby sticks his tongue out to mirror the behavior of a researcher. We are born with the capacity to learn from others.

the understanding that they are somehow like that guy leaning over the crib. Without ever looking in a mirror, they know that they have mouths and tongues like his, and they know how to use them to imitate.

Along with his scientist wife, Patricia Kuhl, Meltzoff directs the Institute for Learning and Brain Sciences at the University of Washington. Kuhl studies what happens in babies' brains as they learn language. She uses the latest technology, including magnetoencephalography, or MEG, to see what is happening inside the brain—in real time.

Understanding Sounds

An oversize helmet attached to the MEG machine fits over a baby's head. Kuhl and her team play sounds that the baby hears through a special set of earphones. Some sounds are simple tones, others are several tones played together in harmony, and still others are human voices.

Just like other body parts, the brain is made up of tiny cells. About a hundred billion of those cells are neurons—special cells that send and receive messages. These messages move fast, activating different parts of the brain as they go. MEG measures these changes as they happen, showing which parts of the brain are active as the baby hears each sound. The point of Kuhl's research is to understand when and how babies know that speech is

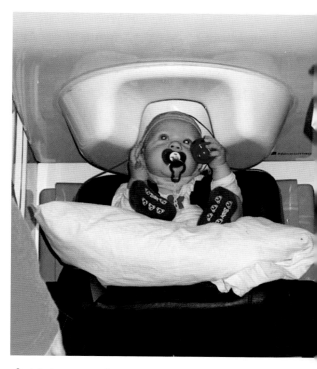

∧ A baby, propped up on a pillow, wearing a helmet attached to a magnetoencephalography (MEG) machine, listens to different sounds. The MEG allows researchers to see what part of the baby's brain corresponds to each noise.

meaningful—that is, different from other types of sound. Are they born knowing it? Is the brain programmed at birth for learning language? Or does the brain change after birth, only later making it possible for babies to learn language?

Inside the Brain

Each area in the brain has its own jobs to do. For example, two areas behind your left forehead help you speak and recognize words. They are called Broca's area and Wernicke's area, named after scientists who studied them. Both of these areas are part of the cerebrum, where people think, remember, and feel.

The cerebrum also controls voluntary muscles, telling your hand to pick up a pencil or to turn a page in a book. A deep groove runs through it from front to back, dividing it into left and right hemispheres. In most people, the left hemisphere controls movement on the right side of the body. The right hemisphere controls the left side. Language is mainly found in the left hemisphere. The right is somewhat involved as well, but less so. The right hemisphere is important for tasks having to do with logic and reasoning, like mathematics, but numbers are decoded by both sides of the brain. The right hemisphere plays a bigger role in understanding the relationship between you and objects around you, and between those objects themselves. The outer part of the cerebrum is called the cortex. It is folded into itself, so that a lot of cortex can fit into the small space it occupies.

The Cerebellum

Below the cerebrum, in the back, is the cerebellum. The cerebellum controls movement, balance, and coordination. When you kick a soccer ball or dance to your favorite song, your cerebellum helps you move without thinking about it much. The brainstem, in front of the cerebellum, connects to your spine. It is a little like an airplane's automatic pilot: it controls the beating of your heart, the movement of air through your lungs, and the digestion of food. These are things your body does without conscious thought.

The Midbrain

The midbrain is the top portion of the brainstem. The midbrain is involved in vision and hearing and in eye movement. Above the midbrain is the diencephalon (including the thalamus and the hypothalamus). The diencephalon works as a sort of relay station, where messages come in and are relayed to other parts of the brain. It also controls some emotions and some "automatic" work, like blood pressure and body temperature.

The Growing, Changing Brain

Babies are born with most of the neurons that they will have as adults, but the neurons are largely unconnected. Every experience forges new connections between

∧ An infant wears a net with electrodes attached to it. This device records electrical activity in his brain.

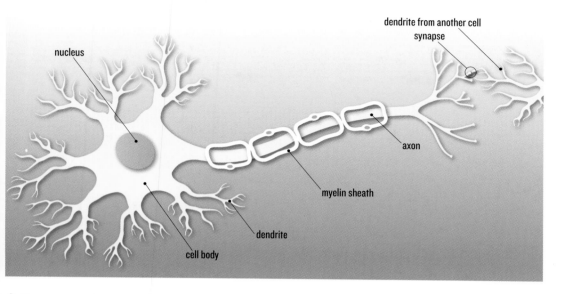

nucleus

dendrite from another cell

synapse

axon

myelin sheath

dendrite

cell body

∧ Neurons contain a nucleus to control the activity of the cell. Dendrites, small structures that branch out around a neuron, carry information across synapses, which create bridges between cells.

neurons. These connections, known as synapses, allow babies to think and feel, to smell, to hear, to see, and to remember. When they experience something more than once or when they see that different experiences are related, the synapses grow more permanent. By two or three years of age, they have more than 15,000 connections for *each* neuron in the brain, probably more than they will have at any other time in life! At that point, the brain begins a sort of cleanup process, thinning out connections. The ones that are not used disappear as the brain "reprograms" itself with each stage of growth.

Between ages three and ten, the brain continues to grow, making new cells and more connections, and thinning them out as needed. Around age ten, just before

adolescence, big changes are happening. Cells multiply quickly, strong connections become stronger, and weaker ones disappear.

By the 18th birthday, connections in the brain have dwindled to 500 trillion—half of what a person has at age three. The brain is a powerhouse—more capable than ever, but less able to pick up new concepts as quickly as the brain of a toddler. Through the late teen years and early to mid-twenties, it continues to transform itself. Areas that think and feel will change the most as the person matures emotionally and intellectually.

The adult brain does not stop changing, but it does not develop as rapidly as it did in childhood. The experiences of life strengthen some parts and prune others. As the person reaches old age, the

Albert Einstein's Brain

As a young child, Albert Einstein, the Nobel Prize-winning scientist, was slow learning to speak. As a teenager, he was fascinated with math, but he found the structure and discipline of school hard to live with. As an adult, he published scientific papers that changed our understanding of physics and the forces that govern life on Earth.

∧ Pieces of Albert Einstein's preserved brain

When Einstein died, he was cremated. His brain, however, was preserved for further research. Over the years, neuroscientists studied Einstein's brain and found that it was a bit unusual. It was smaller than average. The cerebral cortex (used for memory and thought, among other things) was thinner, but denser with neurons—neurons were packed into it more closely together than in an "average" brain. Einstein's parietal lobe, used for mathematical reasoning, was quite large, adding an extra 15% in width to his brain. The brain had other unique traits—every brain is unique, after all—but it is possible that this brain's uniqueness contributed to Einstein's genius.

brain may shrink a bit. Old people's brains are typically lighter and a bit smaller than young adults' brains, but recent research shows that healthy older brains still make new cells and function well.

Language Learning Happens Early

It turns out that babies are not born knowing that words are different from other sounds. Based on Dr. Kuhl's research, the brains of newborn babies become aware in much the same way for all the sounds they hear. To these babies, voices are probably not much different from other tones. Between six months and a year, language-learning parts of the brain begin to respond to the sound of a human voice. These older babies' brains are already learning to use language—a task that most adults find challenging.

Babies learn at their own pace, and some famously bright people have been slow to learn language (Albert Einstein is a good example). On the other hand, difficulties with language can be a warning sign for problems, such as autism. Autism affects the brains of some children, making it hard for them to communicate. Some autistic children never learn to speak or to write. Others speak and even go to school, but have problems understanding other people. They may go through life feeling alone and different. By investigating how babies learn, scientists hope to find early ways to spot children who are having trouble. In the future, scientists may learn to retrain these babies' brains.

Neuroscience Speeds into the Future

Like a control room for a power plant, the brain receives messages from outside and inside the body and then decides what to do with the information. From a protected site inside the skull, brain cells control every feeling, thought, and action— even those that seem automatic, like breathing. Until recently, however, the brain was difficult to study, because much of its work was invisible. Scientists could see a heart beat or a muscle contract, but they could not see a message passing from one brain cell to another. They could not see thought or emotion.

Today, technology is allowing scientists to find their way around the body's control room. Brain-

computer interface (BCI) systems will allow those who are paralyzed or have prosthetic limbs to move parts of their body just by thinking. Brain surgery will become more common as robotic systems enable surgeons to safely operate on areas deep within the brain. As our understanding of neuroscience advances, it will influence medical practice, force the creation of new laws, and create new opportunities to treat illness throughout the body.

∧ **Research on brain development in babies may reveal information about aging brains and diseases that affect brain function.**

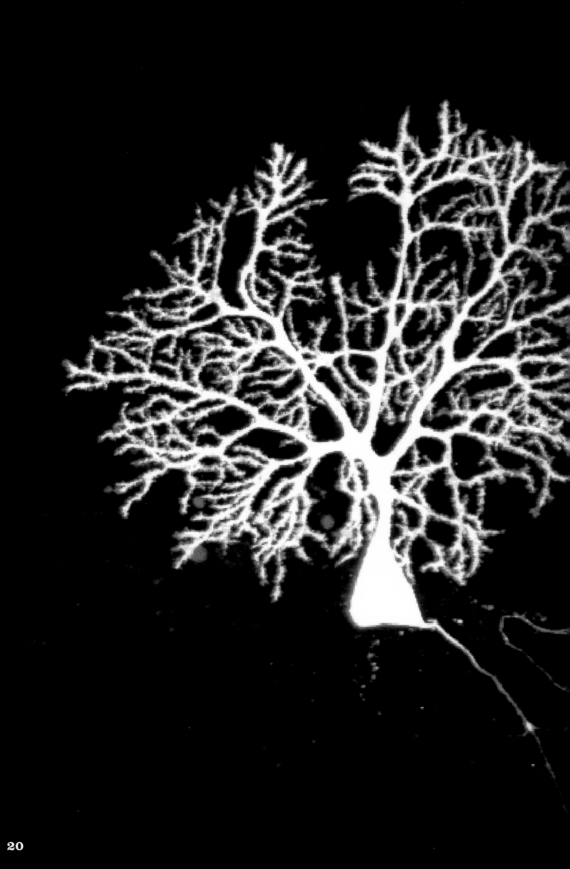

The Language of Neurons

Recording Messages from a Single Cell

The laboratory is quiet. A handful of researchers in blue jeans and T-shirts lean over their microscopes. In the center of this large room, a copper screen surrounds a group of tables with microscopes on them. The screen blocks radio waves that might interfere with electrical equipment. The tables have special legs that work like shock absorbers on a car, so the microscopes will not move if the floor vibrates. At one of these tables, Dr. Bruce Bean peers into a microscope. Carefully, he attaches electrodes to a nerve cell, invisible to the human eye, taken from the brain of a rat. Electrodes usually connect metal

< An image of a sample from a rat's brain shows a neuron that is found in the cerebellum. The portion of the neuron that branches out like a tree is called the dendrite.

to nonmetal, so that electricity can pass from one object to the other. In this case, the electrodes are extremely small, and they are made of glass. Electricity will pass from the nerve cell to a wire. Dr. Bean will use a computer to record that flow. He is studying how the rat's brain cells use electricity to send messages to other cells. In particular, he wants to understand pain messages.

Dr. Bean is part of a team at Harvard Medical School that is working on a new kind of "smart" anesthesia. This anesthesia uses a surprising ingredient: chili peppers! The same chemical that makes peppers hot may someday enable doctors to use anesthesia that has no side effects. It will put patients to sleep without paralyzing them or affecting their memories. All it will do is block pain signals from moving through the body.

The Problem with Anesthesia

Without anesthesia, surgery would be a nightmare, and even a trip to the dentist's office would be pretty unpleasant. In some cases, though, anesthesia itself causes problems. After having a tooth drilled, the patient's mouth feels numb and swollen for hours. Sometimes, dental patients feel sick to their stomachs. In surgery, anesthesia can even cause the patient to stop breathing. The problem is that it blocks more than the pain signals

doctors want it to block. It sometimes shuts down nerve cells that are needed to keep the body working. There is a lot that doctors do not know about anesthesia (why it works, for one thing), but they are learning.

A Little Bit About Neurons

Nerve cells, or neurons, are found in other parts of the body besides the brain. Some are very, very small, and others are as long as your legs. Some send information from the skin, mouth, eyes, ears, and nose to the brain; these are sensory neurons. Others send information from the brain to muscles; these are motor neurons. Still others relay information between sensory and motor neurons; these are interneurons.

Scratch That Itch!

The research into new forms of anesthesia using ingredients found in chili peppers may also help scientists learn about itching and how to treat and prevent its more drastic forms. Although itching is common and usually not serious, in some patients relentless itching can cause serious complications. There are many reasons people may experience this type of reaction, including infection, some forms of cancer, and mental health disorders. Itch-sensitive neurons, however, are much like the neurons that signal pain. Advances in anesthesia may result in relief for people who can't stop scratching!

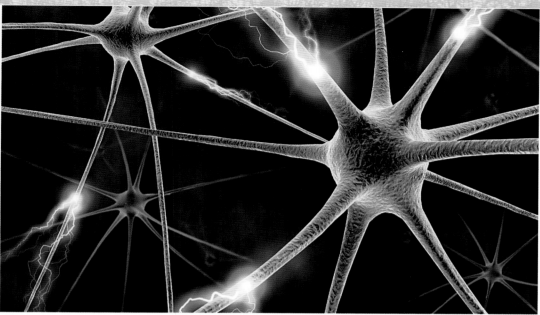

∧ Neurons fire electronic pulses throughout the brain, generating information your body needs to function.

Here is how the process works. First, something happens to trigger a response from neurons. This event is called a stimulus, and it can be pain, heat, flavor, a touch, an odor, or a number of other things. Perhaps you step on a sharp piece of glass. Sensory neurons in your foot fire off a message that cells on the foot are being damaged. This message travels through other neurons, up the spinal cord to the brain. Neurons in the brain respond with a message of their own: pain! Faster than you can consciously think, interneurons relay the brain's messages to other parts of the body. Motor neurons respond. Your heart beats faster. Your muscles tighten. You cry, "Ouch!" and hop around on one foot.

Neurons have a lot in common with other cells. Each has a membrane around it, like a skin. It also has a nucleus—the brain of the cell—that contains genes telling the cell how to do its work. The nucleus exists in the body, or main part, of the cell. Cell bodies make up what is often called "gray matter" in the brain. Unlike other cells, a neuron has dendrites and an axon—wiry parts that help it communicate with other neurons. In the brain, axons make up "white matter." The lighter color of white matter comes from a sheath, or sleeve, of light-colored, fatty tissue that wraps around axons. The sheath is made of myelin, a substance that insulates axons and allows messages to pass quickly from one neuron to the next.

Electric Explosion

Day and night, throughout your life, neurons in your body fire off messages to each other, but how do they communicate? What "language" do neurons use? Since the 1950s,

Animals and Research

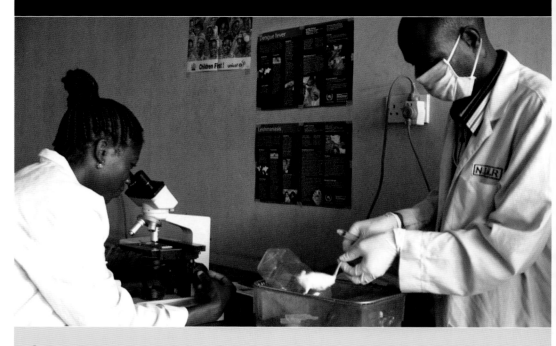

∧ In an effort to learn more about malaria, scientists study how the malaria parasite affects mice. Malaria kills up to two million people around the world each year.

The use of animals in research is becoming less common than it once was, partly because scientists are doing things differently. Researchers now use computers to build models, or simulations, that show how a medicine might work in the body. Another way they can experiment without animals is to grow cells in the laboratory and experiment on those.

Still, according to the Humane Society of the United States, about 20 million animals are used in medical research in the U.S. each year. By far, most of these animals are mice and rats. Their small size, easy handling, and short life span make them ideal for use in laboratory research. Other animals are used as well—cats, pigs, chimpanzees, and ferrets, to name a few. Some people would like to see harmful research on animals stop. They feel it is cruel and unnecessary, pointing to the fact

that technology has made it easier for scientists to do tests without animals. They say that even small animals, such as mice, may suffer more than human researchers can know.

On the other hand, researchers ask how these people would feel if someone they loved suffered from a terrible disease. If these people knew that a new medicine were being tested on mice, one that might treat or even cure that disease, would they want the testing to go on?

Scientists say that animal testing is a necessary part of medical research. Out of all the fields of medicine, neuroscience may have the most to gain from animal research. Animals are used in research to find cures for cancer, mental illness, and many other serious diseases of the brain and nervous system. When they do use animals in experiments, scientists point out there are rules requiring them to treat those animals humanely.

scientists have known that certain chemicals pass through the neuron's cell membrane, creating a small electric pulse. This happens at the dendrites. This pulse moves from one end of the neuron to the other (scientists are unsure exactly how this happens, but they know that it does). When it reaches the end of the axon, the electric pulse triggers a tiny "explosion" of chemicals. Dendrites on nearby neurons detect these chemicals, and the whole process starts over again.

As mentioned in Chapter 1, an adult brain has more than 100 billion neurons, but these are not the only cells in the brain. Glial cells outnumber neurons by more than ten to one. The word *glial* comes from a Greek word for "glue," but these cells do much more than glue neurons together. Glia have several important jobs. They feed neurons, protect them from dangerous bacteria, and even help messages move between neurons. They also hold neurons in place and guide the growth of young brains.

Like an Anesthetic "Smart Bomb"

When the Harvard researchers set out to develop alternate forms of anesthesia, they had a specific goal in mind: to target only those neurons that sense pain. Like a "smart bomb" programmed to strike a specific target, the chili pepper ingredient goes straight to pain-sensing neurons and opens them up to anesthesia.

Then, anesthesia enters only the pain-sensing neurons and shuts them down—no others are affected. Sensory neurons that detect smell, taste, sound, sight, and touch still work. Motor neurons still tell muscles to function. If this research turns out the way the Harvard team expects it to, patients at the dentist's office will be able to speak properly, even after having teeth drilled. Surgical patients will not feel sick to their stomachs. Surgery itself will become less risky, and patients may remain awake during operations. At the moment, the only patients receiving the new anesthesia are rats, but the future of "smart" anesthesia looks promising.

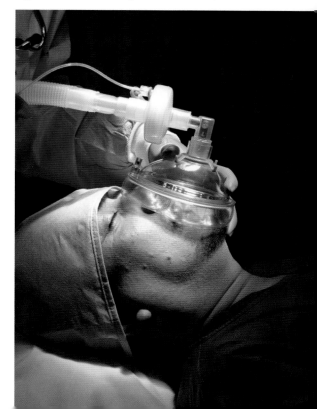

▼ A patient under anesthesia wears a respirator to breathe while a specialist monitors various vital signs to insure the body is not in distress.

Meet a Neuroscientist

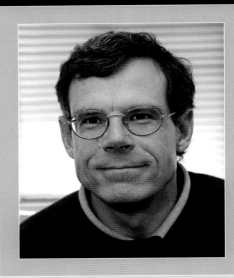

Dr. Bruce Bean is a professor of neurobiology who works at Harvard Medical School. His research involves experiments designed to understand how brain cells use electrical signals to carry information.

◘ What part of your work do you find most interesting or exciting?

▣ Testing an idea by doing an experiment.

◘ When you start to do an experiment, do you know what will happen?

▣ It varies. Sometimes, we'll make a hypothesis—a guess—about how something might work, then try to design an experiment that will test that in some specific way, and then do the experiment and see if it comes out that way. That's often the case, but sometimes we're just exploring, just seeing what the cells do and then trying to think about it.

◘ Are you often surprised?

▣ Yes, being surprised is the best thing. What I like most is if we think we know what's going on, and we have specific predictions about what we're going to see, and then we see something different. That's exciting, actually, because it can show that the way we're thinking about it— maybe the way everybody's thinking about it—is wrong, and there's something we don't understand. That can be a lot of fun.

◘ How did you think of using a chemical from chili peppers in your research?

▣ The actual idea came to me in seconds, but

it depended on odds and ends of information that I had absorbed over many years from reading scientific papers, listening to seminars, and talking with colleagues. This included reading some recently published papers and some recent conversations with colleagues, but also papers I had read 25 years ago as a student.

◘ What is the single most important thing that every preteen or teenager needs to know about the human brain?

▣ The brain is easily damaged by impact to the skull, most commonly in automobile accidents. So always wear seatbelts and drive a little more slowly, and wear a helmet when bicycling, even if it looks a little dorky. Another important thing to know about the brain when you are a teenager is that emotions and impulses are strongly influenced by chemical neurotransmitters and hormones that you have no control over and which are particularly active in teenagers. Strong emotions and mood changes can be difficult to deal with, especially depression. It is important to remember that there is a part of your personality that is purely brain chemistry that you cannot control.

Q So what you are saying is that brain chemistry can make a person feel sad or angry even when nothing has happened to cause those feelings?

A Yes.

Q If you could solve one brain-related mystery, what would it be?

A How we experience and can remember the most powerful emotions, like love.

Q Is there a brain-related myth that you would like to dispel?

A That we only use one-tenth of our brains. We use all of our brain. A lot of it we aren't consciously aware of. For example, catching a baseball or just walking down a flight of stairs requires a huge amount of computation by our brains, as you would realize if you tried to program a robot to do it.

Q What important developments do you see in the near future for neuroscience?

A Better understanding of how mental diseases like schizophrenia and depression develop, and how to prevent or reverse their development.

Q Are we close to preventing and curing those illnesses?

A I would say we're closer to understanding them, and we're closest in the case of depression. I'd say that's going to be a little bit easier to understand and cure than some other brain illnesses. For example, schizophrenia has been an extremely difficult disease to understand.

Q Is there anything else you would like readers to know?

A The brain is especially susceptible to being trained in childhood, adolescence, and early adulthood. So take the opportunity to learn to play a sport you enjoy, or to play a musical instrument, or learn a different language. It will be much easier when you are 15 or 18 than when you are 35 or 40, and what you learn will stay with you for your entire life. Also, by testing your brain in different tasks, you will find what your particular brain is best at.

∧ **Dr. Bruce Bean, left, and other research scientists study computer models of an anesthetized brain.**

The Plastic Brain

London Taxi Drivers and "The Knowledge"

Central London is a maze of one-way streets, narrow alleys, bridges, parks, and construction sites. Thousands of vehicles, from motorcycles to cars to buses, crowd the roads. Among them are the black taxicabs, whose drivers are famous for an encyclopedic knowledge of central London. They know every theater, shop, café, hotel, monument, and office building. They know how to get from one location to the next and what businesses they will pass on the way. In fact, English law requires them to pass a test before receiving a license to drive a taxicab. They spend

< The busy streets of London have always been a challenge for taxi drivers, but research shows their vast knowledge of the geographic area has actually changed their brains.

up to four years studying what they call the Knowledge, taking classes and zipping around central London on scooters or bicycles. Some neuroscientists wondered if memorizing the Knowledge might have a physical effect on the taxi drivers' brains.

People use different parts of their brains for different sorts of tasks. They use one part to make mental "maps" of where things are. It is this task that most interests Eleanor Maguire and her team of London neuroscientists. Using the latest scanning technology, they peer into the brains of London taxi drivers, looking for physical changes brought on by years of mental mapmaking. These changes describe a "plastic" brain, one that changes because of new knowledge or experience.

Looking into a Living Brain

To examine the taxi drivers' brains, Dr. Maguire and her team of scientists at University College London use magnetic resonance imaging (MRI). MRI involves powerful magnets with a concentrated magnetic force stronger than Earth's magnetic field. The magnet in an MRI system is usually about the size of a small bathroom and has a tube through its middle.

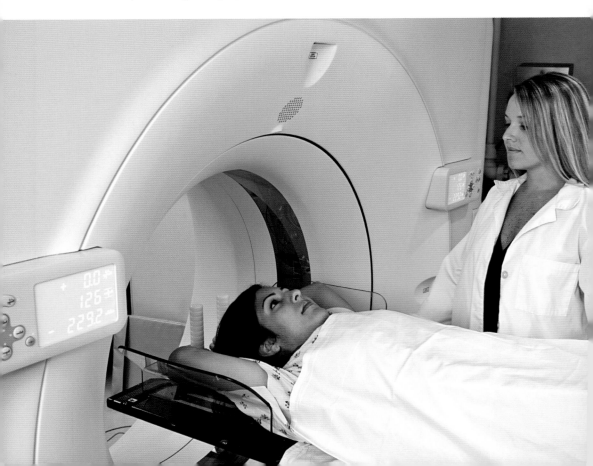

> This picture shows the areas of a London taxi driver's brain that were most active while he participated in a simulation study.

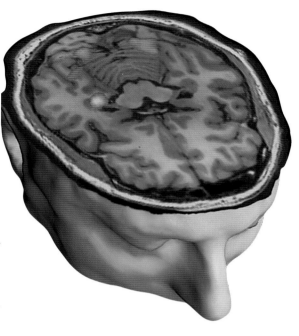

The patient lies on a table that slides in and out of the tube. As the patient lies inside the tube, technicians trigger bursts of radio waves. These cause tiny changes in the positions of particles in the patient's body. Computers record these changes, and the result is a detailed picture of human tissue. For most patients, the procedure is safe, painless, and without side effects.

MRI technology has transformed brain science. Scientists can point the device at deeply buried areas of the brain to study and measure them. MRI offers a cross section of any part of the brain so that doctors see several areas at once.

Alternative Technologies

Today's neuroscientists have several other tools for looking into a living brain. Electroencephalography (EEG) records electrical activity in the brain. Wires run from electrodes placed on the patient's head to a machine. The machine makes a graph showing changes in brain activity. Computed tomography (CT) scans use X-ray science to see through the skull. Cross-section images of the brain appear on film. CT scans give doctors a picture of the brain's structure, but tell them nothing about brain activity. To see a picture of how the brain is working, doctors can use positron emission tomography (PET) scans or functional MRI (fMRI). For a PET scan, radioactive material is injected into a vein or inhaled. The material travels to active parts of the brain and breaks down. A gamma ray detector "sees" gamma rays that are released as the radioactive material breaks down. The resulting picture shows which areas of the brain are active. Functional MRI works much like a PET scan, but also measures changes in blood flow. Parts of the brain with lots of blood flow are highly active at the time of the fMRI.

< A patient prepares to enter a magnetic resonance imaging (MRI) machine. The painless procedure has increased scientists' knowledge of the workings of the brain more than any other technology developed so far.

Seahorsepower

Dr. Maguire and her team study MRI scans of the hippocampus, an area of the brain that helps people find their way around and remember past experiences. The brain has two hippocampi, right and left, lying deep within the brain. Each hippocampus has a curling shape that ancient doctors thought looked like a seahorse. The word *hippocampus* comes from Greek words meaning "seahorse."

When Dr. Maguire's team compared the MRIs of taxi drivers' brains to London bus drivers' brains, they made some startling discoveries. The structure of the hippocampus was different in the taxi drivers; the back part was larger than in the other brains. In fact, the longer the taxi drivers had been on the job, the larger this area of the brain was. At the same time, the front part of the hippocampus was smaller, possibly to make room for growth at the back.

Next, the scientists gave a series of tests to both the taxi drivers and the bus drivers. On tests covering only landmarks of central London, taxi drivers performed far better than bus drivers. On the other hand, the taxi drivers did not do as well when asked to remember new information. The taxi drivers seem to have made a trade-off: The hippocampus devoted extra space to processing long-term "navigating" memory. It gave up space that would be used for learning new information.

What Is Memory?

Think about your earliest memory. It may be the feeling of sunshine on your bare shoulders. It may be the

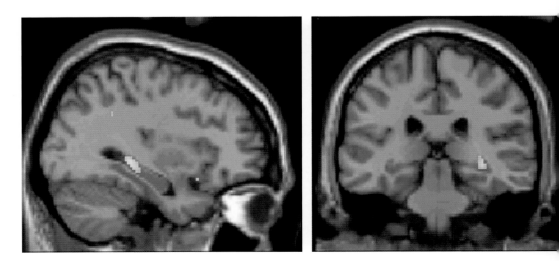

∧ The highlighted areas of this image of a London taxi driver's brain indicate a hippocampus that is larger than those of a London bus driver's.

Music and the Brain

∧ Mastering an instrument while you are young may be good for your grades!

Can music change the brain? Can it make you smarter? A number of studies have asked that question, but no one has formulated a solid answer. In 1995, a neuroscientist named Gottfried Schlaug studied the brains of musicians. He learned that the brains of most musicans were built differently from the brains of nonmusicians. The corpus callosum, a rope of tissue that connects the right and left sides of the brain, was bigger in most of the musicians. This allowed the two halves of the brain to "talk" to each other more efficiently. Schlaug was not sure if the large corpus callosum was a cause or an effect: Did these people become musicians because the corpus callosum was bigger, or did the corpus callosum grow because of their musical practice?

So he did another study. This time, he made MRI images of children's brains at age six and then again at age nine. Some of the children practiced a musical instrument at least two and a half hours each week, and others did not. After the second set of MRI images, the corpus callosum had grown more in the children who practiced every day. They performed better at certain tasks, such as two-handed work at a computer keyboard. Schlaug is continuing his investigation, observing the children to see how their memory and reasoning skills improve.

face of a parent, smiling in a crowd of unfamiliar faces. But what is memory? Memory seems to live in the connections between neurons. It is how people receive, interpret, store, and recall information—all kinds of information. The memories described above involve long-term memory, information that is stored in the brain for later use.

There are other types of memory. Working memory (also called short-term memory) is the phone number you try to remember as your new friend recites it for you.

It is the list of page numbers your teacher calls out when assigning homework. Working memory lasts a few seconds—unless you extend it by repeating information over and over—and then the information is committed to long-term memory, or forgotten. Working memory does not hold much information, and the information that it does hold is easy to forget.

Then there is sensory memory, the briefest of them all. Sensory memory is the quick flash of a face you have just seen or a sound you have just heard. It may involve your sense of taste, touch, or smell, too. It lasts anywhere from one to four seconds, but you are not usually aware of it; you do not think about it at all. It just happens, a sort of echo of an experience.

Keeping Your Brain Fit

There are things you can do to sharpen your memory. One of the most important is to exercise your brain. Learn new things. Read new books. Enjoy new experiences. Experts believe that using parts of the brain that work on memory and learning strengthens the connections between neurons. Stronger connections should mean a better memory. Memory tricks can help, too. To remember a list of names, you might try making an acronym.

< Just as it is important to keep your body fit, it is important to your brain's health to exercise it throughout your life.

∧ In the past scientists believed the adult brain did not change, but research has shown that by keeping fit, the brains of adults and even elderly people can grow stronger.

Let's say you want to remember the names of the Great Lakes. You could take the first letter from each name and put them all together to make a word, like HOMES: Huron, Ontario, Michigan, Erie, Superior. Some people write down everything they want to remember. Just the act of writing may strengthen connections in your brain enough so you will remember. If not, you can check your notes later. Relax. Stress affects memory-related parts of the brain in negative ways. Exercise and eat right. Studies show that exercise and nutritious food increase blood flow to memory-related areas in the brain. This seems to encourage cell growth and improve memory.

The Adult Brain

For a long time, scientists thought that adult brains did not change much, other than changes caused by disease. Most scientists believed that only young brains were plastic. However, the taxi drivers' brains changed after learning the Knowledge, proving that they were plastic. Dr. Maguire's discovery that even adult brains are plastic offers hope for people whose brains have been damaged by injury or disease.

It means that healthy parts of the brain might be able to change their structure and to make up for unhealthy parts. It also means that adults might be able to strengthen parts of their brains just by using them more.

35

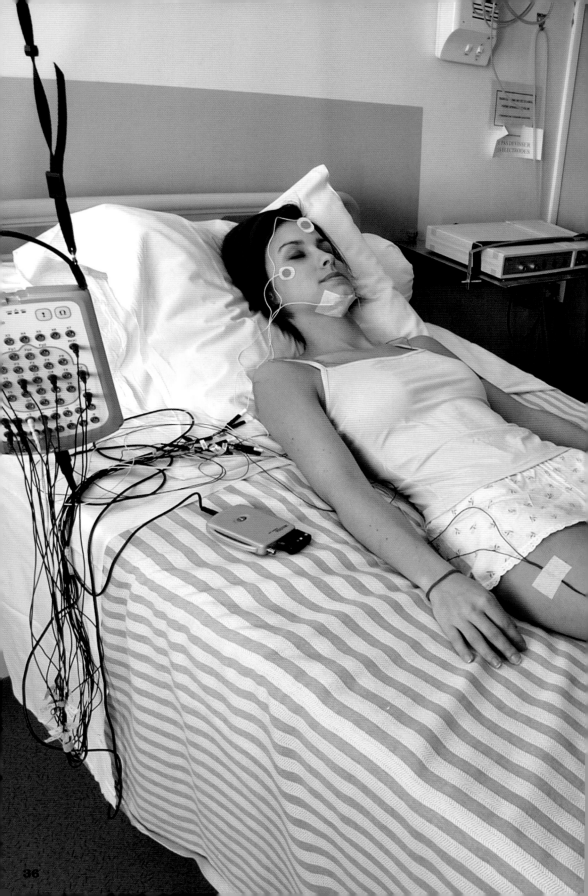

Sleep and Dreams

No Time Off

In math, you practice using formulas to solve problems. In language arts, you learn how to write poetry in the Japanese style. After school, you finally manage to put the ball through the hoop from the free throw line. You eat dinner, do your homework, and fall asleep listening to your favorite music. But wait. Your day is not over yet. While you sleep, your brain is hard at work, making sense of skills that you learned when you were awake.

Sleepers drift through four stages of sleep, each one deeper than the one before. During stage 1, you are sleeping lightly and can be awakened easily. In stage 2, your eyes stop moving and the amount of rapid brain waves (electrical activity within your

< **Research conducted in sleep labs has shown that the brain never completely shuts down. Sensors attached to various parts of the body record information such as eye movement, breathing, and brain activity, which gives scientists insight into our health.**

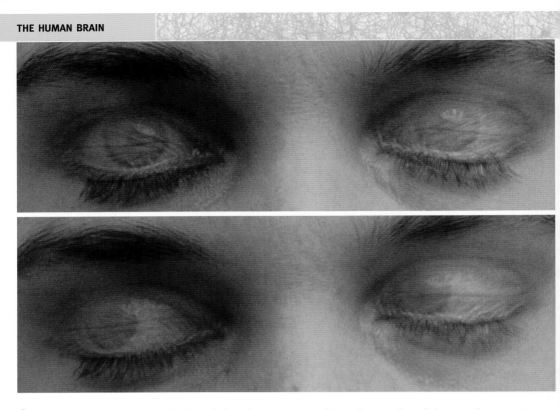

∧ A photograph of a person sleeping during the REM stage shows the muscles of the eyes in constant motion behind closed lids.

brain) decreases greatly. Stages 3 and 4 are called slow wave sleep (SWS) because the brain generates very slow waves. After stage 4, your brain begins to speed up again. You go backward through the stages until you enter something called rapid eye movement, or REM sleep. During REM sleep, limbs are paralyzed and eyes move in quick bursts of activity. This is when much, but not all, dreaming occurs. The sleep cycle—"downward" through the four stages to deep sleep, then "upward" through the stages and REM sleep—lasts about an hour and a half. Sleepers repeat the cycle several times a night.

Scientists have lots of questions about sleep. Clearly, people need to sleep, but why? What does sleep do for the body and mind? And why do people dream? Does sleep affect learning? Robert Stickgold, a professor at Harvard Medical School, looks for answers to questions like these. To find them, he works with a team of volunteers who learn something and then sleep on it.

Learning in Their Sleep

Stickgold teaches his volunteers a skill, such as tapping out a series of numbers on a keyboard. After practicing for a while, the volunteers can do the task quickly and with few mistakes. When he tests them several hours later, their speed has not improved, but it has not slowed down, either. Then

Stickgold lets them sleep. The next day, he tests them again. Even though they have not practiced overnight, the volunteers get better at the task after sleeping—about 20 percent better.

How Much Sleep Do People Need?

To keep neurons properly zapping messages back and forth in the brain, people need sleep. No two people are put together in exactly the same way, though. How much sleep they need will differ from one person to the next. Doctors do offer guidelines, based on age. Newborn babies are marathon sleepers—they snooze as much as 20 hours out of every 24. Young children between three and five years of age sleep a lot, too, usually 11 to 13 hours in a day. Between 5 and 12 years of age, children sleep a bit less—10 or 11 hours per night. Most adults need seven or eight hours of sleep.

The average teenager needs at least nine hours of sleep, but many teens have a hard time getting that much. They feel a burst of energy around ten or eleven at night, so they do not want to go to bed. At seven the next morning, when the alarm clock goes off, teens groan and pull pillows over their heads. Their brains want more sleep. The problem involves circadian rhythms.

Circadian comes from Latin words that mean "about a day." Living things follow a cycle of

What Happens if People Don't Get Enough Sleep?

⋀ **Sleepwalking occurs during non-REM slow wave phases of sleep earlier in the sleep cycle.**

Lack of sleep is a dangerous business that can cause problems ranging from car wrecks to illness and even hallucinations. Here are a few things that are more difficult to accomplish when a person is sleepy:

- Thinking clearly and making decisions
- Fighting off disease—lack of sleep weakens the immune system
- Playing sports or games—lack of sleep slows reaction time and affects coordination
- Driving a car
- Having fun—lack of sleep affects mood

Recent research seems to show a link between mental illness and sleep debt, but the exact nature of the link is unclear. Does mental illness keep patients from sleeping, or does lack of sleep contribute to mental illness? Doctors have not been able to answer that question.

wakefulness and sleep that is about a day in length. To keep them on this cycle, they have a sort of internal clock. In humans, the clock is located about 1.2 inches (3 cm) behind the eyes, in a part of the brain known as the hypothalamus. This internal clock tells the rest of the brain when to feel sleepy, when to wake up, and when to feel active.

Sometime around ten or eleven years of age, the circadian rhythms of many children change. No one knows why these changes happen, but they last throughout the teenage years and into the early twenties, making it difficult for teenagers to get enough sleep. Those hours of missed sleep pile up, creating a new problem: sleep debt. Sleep debt is more than morning sluggishness. Sleep debt is accumulated hours of missed sleep. Sleep debt is not "paid back" over time, although you may end up sleeping one or two extra hours for a few days after accumulating sleep debt.

The Dreaming Brain

REM dreams seem very vivid, almost real. When woken from REM sleep, most people can recall their dreams—even small details. REM sleep is a lot like wakefulness; certain parts of the brain become very active. The imagination is active, and so is the part that controls emotions. The part of the brain that thinks logically turns down, leading to sometimes bizarre dreams. During REM sleep, the five senses cannot send messages to the brain. The senses work, but "gatekeeping" neurons that control information going in and out of the brain refuse to let sensory messages pass. The same thing happens when the REM-sleeping brain tries to send messages to arms and legs. The gatekeeping neurons will not let action messages pass from the brain to the rest of the body. The sleeper is largely paralyzed. Breathing and heartbeat become less regular. The REM sleeper's body temperature rises and falls with room temperature.

REM sleep is no longer a complete mystery to scientists, but dreams are another matter. There have been lots of theories about why people dream. Some experts believe that people dream about things that

< One out of three Americans has sleep issues. Developing healthy sleeping patterns as a young adult can prevent sleep and health problems as you age.

Other than those with injured brains, everyone dreams. Any pet owner can tell you that even animals dream. Laboratory rats who have learned a route through a maze seem to dream about the route afterward. Researchers record brain activity while the rats are learning the route and again while the animals sleep. The recordings show that the same parts of the brain become active and in the same order. Of course, this does not prove that the rats dream about the maze, but it seems likely.

To Cram or Not to Cram

An interesting part of Dr. Stickgold's research involves volunteers who do not sleep after learning a skill. They learn the same task as the first set of volunteers. They practice it and their skills improve. When they are retested hours later—after the same amount of nonpractice time that the sleepers had—they do not get better at it. Even if they come back two days later, their scores do not improve the way the sleepers' scores did. They seem to have missed an opportunity to learn by not "sleeping on the problem." Dr. Stickgold believes that sleep is key to learning, and remembering, certain types of things. So should you stay up late cramming for a big test, or should you sleep? Look at it this way: Sleeping might help you do better on the test. Even if it does not, you will feel better after a good night's sleep.

∧ **Some school districts are considering changing the day's schedule to accommodate the different sleep cycles of elementary school children and middle and high school kids.**

they want. Others think dreams are like a yard sale in the brain—a way of getting rid of useless information to make room for new, needed information. Still others have said that dreams serve no real purpose at all; they are just a side effect of sleep.

Some people are unable to dream. These people suffer from a disease or have had a stroke that damaged brain tissue needed for dreaming. (A stroke happens when blood flow to part of the brain is blocked.) Usually, the damage causes other symptoms, like loss of vision, but not always.

CHAPTER 5

Happiness and the Brain

Mind Control!

In a laboratory at the University of Wisconsin, a Buddhist monk sits perfectly still, his eyes slightly open. Wires run from electrodes on his head to an EEG machine. The monk is awake, but he is meditating—focusing his mind on kind and compassionate thoughts, wishing for the happiness and well-being of others. Although his body is still, his brain is active. Especially active is the part where he feels positive emotions, including happiness. This monk has learned to change what happens inside his brain—he has trained his brain for positive feelings. By learning about meditation through the people who practice it, neuroscientists are forming new ideas about human thought and behavior.

< Buddhist monks pray in Indonesia. Many Buddhists are practiced meditators. Their techniques have opened up a new form of brain research into what makes people happy.

Happy Brains of Buddhist Meditators

Scientists have known for some time that what happens in the brain affects the way people think and feel. Illness or injury in the brain can cause feelings of anger, sadness, and hopelessness. Richard Davidson, a professor of psychiatry and psychology at the University of Wisconsin, shows that the opposite is true, too: Thoughts can change the way the brain works.

Davidson has asked a group of people from Tibet, Buddhists who

∇ Buddhist meditators spend years mastering the technique that allows them to control their thoughts and to focus on specific ideas for long periods of time.

∇ Dr. Richard Davidson during a conference discussing the effects of meditation on happiness. The Dalai Lama is an expert on various methods of meditation.

have long experience in meditation, to help him study the human brain. Buddhists are people who follow the religious ideas of an ancient teacher named Siddhartha Gautama. This teacher is known as the Buddha, a name that means "enlightened one." The Buddhists who meditate in Davidson's laboratory believe that people can control their minds through meditation—training the mind to focus on specific thoughts for long periods of time. Their work includes more than 10,000 hours spent in meditation, and they have become experts at it.

To find out how all this meditation might affect the brain, Dr. Davidson's team makes EEG recordings of the experienced meditators' brain activity. The results are dramatic. In an area of the brain that calms fear and produces good feelings, meditation sets off broad waves of intense activity.

Next, the team members teach a group of volunteers to meditate as the long-term Buddhist meditators do, focusing their minds on compassion and kindness. In the beginning, the volunteers meditate on compassion and kindness toward friends and family. As training goes on, they broaden their thoughts, meditating on compassion and kindness toward all people. When researchers make EEG recordings of these meditating brains, activity in the happiness areas of the brain again ramps up. They are clearly more active than before the volunteers began meditating

∧ Buddhist monks begin training in childhood. Most have become experts at meditation by the time they are young adults.

(although not as active as in the experienced meditators' brains). Even when they are not meditating, these parts of the Buddhists' brains are more active than in the volunteers' brains. Could it be that people can train their brains for happiness?

An Emotional Brain

Emotions are universal. No one teaches you to be fearful, angry, or happy; feelings are basic to survival. Fear tells you to run away from danger, anger tells you to fight for your life, and love creates a need for connection.

Several things happen in the brain when you feel emotions. Neurons in the limbic system, which includes the frontal cortex, the amygdala, and a few other parts, start zapping messages back and forth.

Λ **Happy people are often those who give and receive love freely, do things for others, set goals, and share their beliefs with others.**

First, sensory neurons (smell, taste, sight, touch, or sound) tell the brain that something is happening. Deep brain areas, such as the amygdala, give you "gut reactions." This happens in the oldest, most primitive parts of the brain, which all animals need for survival. The frontal cortex is a more sophisticated part of the brain that developed as humans evolved. This area thinks over the messages that your senses send to it. Then it shoots messages off to those primitive parts. It may calm them, squashing a gut reaction of fear or anger, or it may tell them to react in some other way. In Dr. Davidson's

studies, meditation triggers activity in the frontal cortex and in the pathways that carry calming messages to the fearful amygdala.

A wide range of emotions is important for human survival, but sometimes the systems that control emotions can go haywire. Fear can take over people's lives so that they become afraid to do the simplest things. Sadness can become dark, dangerous depression. Pleasure can become addictive behavior. At present, scientists do not understand mental illnesses like these very well, but with the help of brain-scanning technology, they are learning more every day.

Happiness Is...

So what makes people happy? To find out, psychologists need a way to measure how happy people are. In large part, they do this by asking, "On a scale of one to ten, how happy are you?" This method may not seem very scientific, but some psychologists say that it gives them accurate answers.

Choosing to Be Happy

⋀ Children who practice "happiness" skills when they are young will likely carry these feelings into adulthood.

Buddhists believe that happiness is something you can work to get better at—a skill, like skating or writing. Scientists say there are things you can do to boost your happiness skills:

- Exercise makes the brain release chemicals that cause you to feel good, at least for a little while. Exercise is an important part of staying healthy, and it may enhance long-term happiness as well.

- Psychologists say that it is important to spend time with other people. This may deepen relationships that are important to both you and others.

- Gratitude—thankfulness—can increase happiness, too. Every day, think about good things that have occurred in your life. Write thank-you notes or tell people in person how much you appreciate what they have done for you.

- Identify your strengths—qualities like kindness, courage, and fairness. Then use those strengths to work toward goals that matter to you.

For one thing—and most children know this, even if adults sometimes forget—friends matter. People need to love and be loved, so the happiest people have good relationships with friends and family. On the other hand, money is not as important as you might think. If people have enough money to feel safe (enough to pay for food, health care, and a safe place to live), more does not necessarily bring greater happiness. Also, the happiest people have meaning in their lives, whether it comes from religion or a way of looking at the world. They believe in something greater than themselves. Psychologists say that goals are important, too. People gain happiness from setting goals and then working to achieve them.

Programmed for Emotion

Genes may be most important of all in the pursuit of a happy life. Genes exist

in the nucleus of a cell, and they carry instructions for how each cell should grow and do its work. They direct development of each living thing, telling it to become a frog or a human, a chicken or a giraffe. They tell the hair to grow in brown and straight instead of red and curly. They even tell some people to be athletic, musical, or grumpy, and others to be awkward, creative, or cheerful. Genes do not run the whole show—other factors, such as diet, geography, and upbringing, also influence how people feel and behave—but genes are important. Some people are just programmed to be happier than others. They shrug off disappointments and look forward to a better day.

Dr. Davidson's team put fMRI technology to work in their study. A long-term Buddhist meditator lies on his back, his body partly inside an enormous fMRI machine. While researchers study images of his brain, he hears recorded sounds: a crying child, people talking in a restaurant, and so on. This time, the team is trying to understand how the brain processes empathy and compassion and how meditation affects those feelings. When the recordings are played, the meditator's brain lights up in areas that handle emotions. The other volunteers, with less meditation training than the Buddhists, light up the fMRI in the same way, but

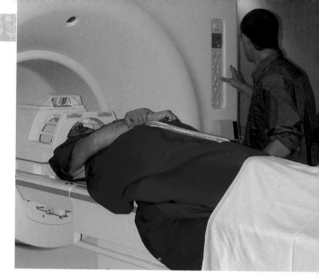

∧ A long-term Buddhist meditator prepares to undergo an MRI. The MRI will illustrate how the brain reacts when the patient has different emotions.

not quite as much as the experienced meditators do. It is possible that meditation has a quieting affect on negative emotions by strengthening the neurological switches that turn these emotions off. So what does all this mean to you? It means that you can train your brain, just like the volunteers. If your parents, aunts, uncles, and cousins are all really grouchy, you may never be as cheerful, compassionate, or serene as a long-term Buddhist meditator. You can maximize good feelings, though, with practice. It also follows that meditation can affect our behavior. Perhaps meditation could take the place of medication for people who have been diagnosed with depression. Widespread meditation might even lead to a more peaceful society. This exciting area of neuroscience and our ability to control our minds holds great promise.

< Most experts agree that happiness takes work! The happiest people put effort into activities that bring them fulfillment.

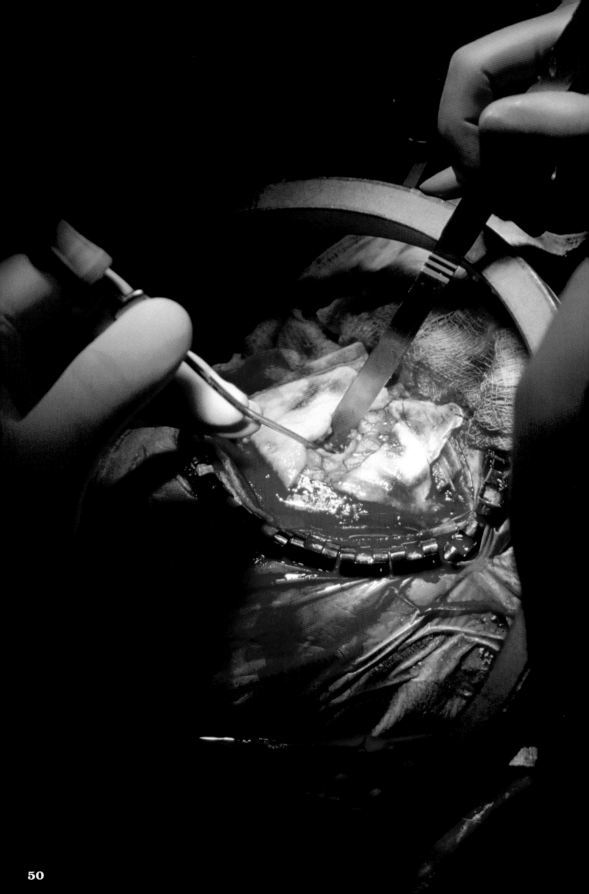

Operating on the Brain

Surgeons Reawaken an Injured Brain

In 1999, muggers attacked a man in his early 30s. They crushed his skull, robbed him, and left him to die. He nearly did die—but not quite. For the next six years, the man lay somewhere between consciousness and coma. His damaged brain was unable to send instructions to his body. He could not chew or swallow—liquid nutrition flowed into him through tubes. Sometimes, he was able to move his eyes or fingers to answer yes or no questions. Other times, he could not do even that. He was minimally conscious.

< All brain operations carry great risk, but new hi-tech tools allow doctors to perform surgery that would have been too dangerous in the past.

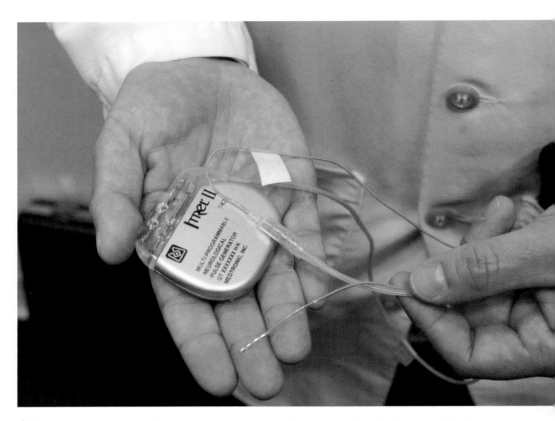

∧ This stimulation device allows doctors to activate portions deep within the brain. In DBS (deep brain stimulation) doctors implant this device, which sends electronic pulses to target areas within the brain.

Scientists do not understand consciousness very well, but they generally suggest that conscious patients are awake, and their deliberate actions show that they are aware. Minimally conscious patients sometimes show signs of being awake and aware, but not always. They may not be able to move much, but they might occasionally perform deliberate actions, such as moving a finger in answer to a question. Patients in a coma, by contrast, show no sign of being aware. They may appear to be asleep, but they do not wake if someone speaks to them or shakes their shoulder.

In the years since the mugged man's injury, doctors and neuroscientists at Weill Cornell Medical College and the Cleveland Clinic worked on an exciting, new kind of surgery. It is called deep brain stimulation (DBS). It involves boring through the patient's skull and inserting electrodes deep into the brain. The electrodes are connected to wires that run under the skin to a pacemaker implanted in the chest. The pacemaker sends tiny electric pulses to the brain. The Cleveland team had used the surgery to treat patients with certain diseases, and results had been encouraging. Doctors hoped that DBS would wake up the injured man's brain, helping weakened parts work better.

Brain Surgery

In brain surgery, a cut one millimeter in the wrong direction could make a patient unable to speak or to move. To address this problem, patients are often awake for part of the surgery. Doctors begin by making a "map" of the brain. Global positioning system (GPS) technology can now be used, along with MRI, to make mapping extremely precise. (GPS technology allows users to find precise locations and directions to a destination. Satellites broadcast signals that receivers on Earth can pick up. Experts have adapted the technology for brain surgery, so doctors can navigate their way around the brain with great precision.) The patient's head is held in place with a large vise to keep it from moving. A dose of anesthesia puts the patient to sleep during the first part of the operation. Surgeons

cut through the skin on the scalp and then open a hole in the skull. They remove a piece of the skull, called a bone flap, and cut through the dura mater, a protective layer of tissue between the skull and the brain.

When doctors are ready to work on the brain itself, they may wake the patient by lowering the level of anesthesia. A wide-awake patient can guide surgeons through the brain. For example, surgeons may intend to remove a tumor near a part of the brain used for language. They probe tissue that they want to cut out. Then, they show the patient a flash card. If the patient can name the object pictured on the card, the doctors know that specific tissue does not trigger language; it is okay to cut there. Cutting does not hurt the patient, because the brain does not have the type of neurons that sense pain. Doctors can poke and cut, and the patient remains comfortable, maybe even a little bored.

< A brain surgery patient before an operation has markers attached to the skin so doctors know exactly where to cut. This increases the accuracy of the operation and reduces the risk of damage to the brain.

Ancient Brain Surgery

It takes a certain daring to open the skull of a living person. Apparently, there have always been people in the world with such daring, because some of the first surgeries ever performed were on the brain. As early as 7,000 years ago, people with wounds to the head received brain surgery—probably without anesthesia—and survived! At a burial site in France, scientists found an ancient skull that had been opened not once, but twice. The patient's first brain surgery, which doctors today would call a craniotomy, had completely healed. The second surgery had partially healed when the man died at about age 50. Scientists say this skull dates to the late Stone Age, around 5,000 B.C. Thousand-year-old skulls found in Peru show signs of having been operated on, too, but with less success. Many of the early Peruvian skulls do not show signs of healing, indicating that the patients died. Later, in the time of the Incas, Peruvian surgeons learned better techniques, and most of their patients survived. Ancient Egyptians, Romans, Greeks, Chinese, and Indians also operated on the brain. Experts are not sure why ancient people performed brain surgeries. It may have been done to treat head wounds, mental illness, or disease. On the other hand, it could have been done to get rid of evil spirits believed to live in the patient's body.

⋀ The skeleton of a young woman from the third century A.D. found in northern Greece has a large hole in the front of the skull, likely from brain surgery nearly 1,800 years ago.

Protection for the Fragile Brain

The skull works like a suit of armor for the brain. A baby is born with a skull made of cartilage plates, but as the child matures, so does the skull. In time, the cartilage turns to bone, and most of the plates grow together. An adult skull is made up of 22 bones: 14 of them make up the face, while the other 8 fit together to form the cranium. The cranium protects the brain from bumps. When a baby is born, the cranium is not completely formed. It has soft spots called fontanels, which allow the head to change shape during birth. This makes it easier for the baby to move through the mother's body. By two years of age, bones have knit together and the fontanels have disappeared.

Inside the skull, a layer of fluid offers more protection for the brain. Beneath that, tough layers of tissue cover the brain and spinal cord, so they will not rub against bone. The brain needs food, oxygen, and water, so a network of blood vessels delivers them, first filtering out harmful chemicals. This filter, called the blood-brain barrier, allows food, oxygen, and water to pass through the walls of blood vessels into the brain. When chemicals that might harm the brain try to pass through, the blood-brain barrier blocks them.

Surgery for the Mugging Victim

In 2005, surgeons at the Cleveland Clinic performed DBS on the brain of the man who had been attacked. Doctors had to be careful about operating on this man. The surgery was not needed to save his life, and it was experimental—it had never been done on a brain-injured patient before. Normally, patients are legally required to give permission for surgery, but this patient was not able to give it because his brain was too seriously injured. So the surgeons asked for permission from his family and for approval from the government.

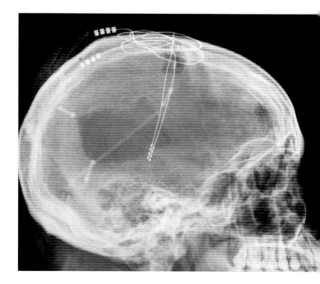

∧ An X-ray illustrates electrodes placed within the brain of an injured man. The electrodes stimulate areas of the brain that allow him to talk, eat, and move parts of his body.

With the go-ahead from both family and the federal government, doctors performed the surgery. It took ten hours. They drilled a small hole in the patient's skull and placed electrodes on his thalamus, an area deep in his brain. According to Dr. Ali Rezai, one of the surgeons involved, the thalamus is a little like a busy train station. Signals come into it from the eyes, ears, nose, and so on, and the thalamus relays them to the other parts of the brain. If the thalamus is not working, other parts do not receive all the signals they need in order to function properly. The surgeons then connected the electrodes to a pacemaker implanted in the man's chest.

After the operation, doctors spent months fine-tuning the electrical pulses that the pacemaker sent to the man's brain. The pacemaker can be programmed to work in thousands of different ways, so—it was important to find programming that was best for this patient. Now, the man

▽ Surgeons at the Cleveland Clinic perform DBS surgery on a patient. The advantages of DBS include the lack of trauma to other areas of the brain. A disadvantage is that repeat surgeries may be required every few years to replace batteries in the device.

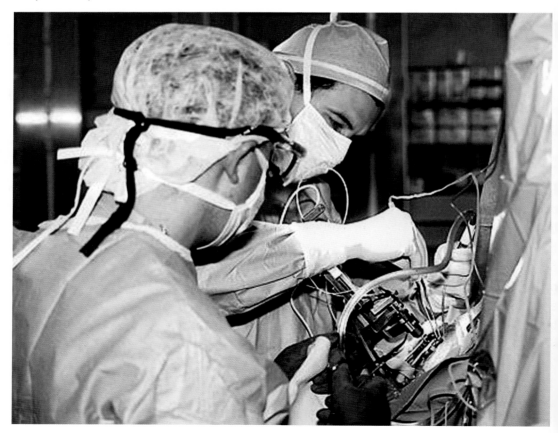

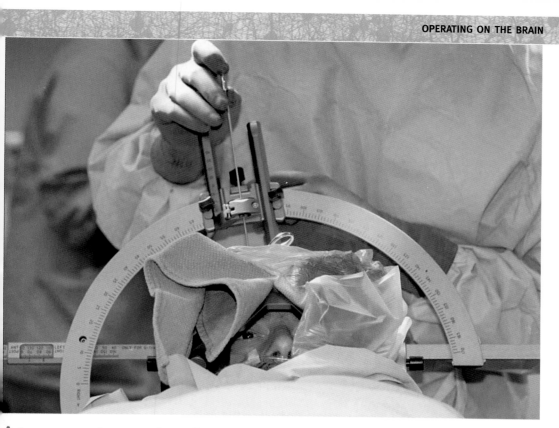

Λ A surgeon operates on a patient suffering from Parkinson's disease. The patient remains awake during the five-hour procedure.

chews his food, can move his arms and legs, and speaks short sentences. When his mother walks into the room, he says, "Hello."

New Reasons for Hope

In the United States, many thousands of brain-injured patients live out their lives in nursing homes, unable to talk to doctors or family. For many, there has been no hope that their lives would ever improve—until now. Today, brain surgery treats a wide range of problems, including tumors (harmful cell growth) in the brain, disease, and injury. Deep brain stimulators like the one used at the Cleveland Clinic treat severe

depression, Parkinson's disease, and obsessive-compulsive disorder (OCD), a disorder that causes a person to repeat the same actions, such as washing hands or looking over a shoulder, over and over again.

New techniques in fMRI also provide brain surgeons with the ability to pinpoint brain disorders that may have gone unseen in the past. Surprisingly, some researchers believe fMRI can provide evidence that non-communicative patients in long-term comas may even have brain patterns indicating awareness. Science must cautiously explore these new frontiers. The future looks promising, however, for many who had given up hope in the past.

The Years Ahead

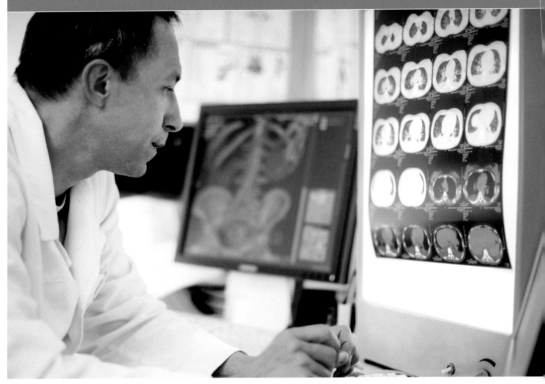

∧ Doctors and researchers who study brain cells must figure out ways to apply new technologies in order to best serve mankind.

Neuroscientists are now faced with another huge challenge. The success of DBS raises the question, what other problems could DBS help with? Because the brain is the body's control center, problems there can affect all other parts of the body. This means that many problems in the body might be treated in the brain. As neuroscientists learn more about the brain, they will find ways to treat problems that once were not treatable. Children with autism may be trained to understand and connect with the world around them. Doctors may discover how to relieve pain more safely. Adults may be trained to stretch their plastic brains, making life more interesting. As scientists study sleep and dreams, students may become better learners. One day, parents may train themselves and their children to be happier. The horror of mental illness may lessen, as doctors learn to treat it more effectively. People with damaged brains—a problem that grows in times of war, as soldiers come home with head injuries—may find relief. These are high hopes, but they are not out of the reach of science.

Glossary

adolescence — the process of growing to maturity

anesthetic — a drug that stops pain

cartilage — connective tissue found in various parts of the body

cell — the smallest unit of life

circa — approximately

communicate — to send or exchange information

cross section — an angled "slice" that allows a view of the brain's internal structure

electrode — a device that allows electricity to pass between metal and nonmetal

fluid — something that can flow, such as water

glands — organs that discharge a substance

hemispheres — the two halves of the brain

magnetic field — a magnetic buffer that surrounds much of the planet Earth

navigate — to find the way from one place to another

neuron — a nerve cell; a cell that relays information to or from the brain or spinal cord

neuroscientist — a scientist who studies the brain

nucleus — the part of a cell that controls how it functions, sometimes known as the "brain" of the cell

plastic — referring to a brain that responds to environmental change

psychologist — a scientist who studies human behavior and the mind

radioactive — giving off energy in the form of waves or particles

real time — the actual time during which a process is taking place

sensory — having to do with the five senses

sleep debt — the hours of sleep one loses over time

spinal cord — a rope of nerve tissue that runs from the brain down the backbone

surgery — medical treatment in which doctors cut into the body

tissue — cells that are part of a plant or animal

tumor — a clump of abnormal cells

vibrate — to shake

voluntary — willful; done out of a deliberate choice

Bibliography

Books

Burrell, Brian. *Postcards from the Brain Museum*. New York: Broadway Books, 2005.

Articles

Science Illustrated. "A Sound Theory." May/June 2008.

Harvard Medical School, Office of Public Affairs. "Researchers Develop Targeted Approach to Pain Management." October 3, 2007.

http://web.med.harvard.edu/sites/ RELEASES/html/Oct07Pain.html. (Accessed August 13, 2008.)

On the Web

Harvard Brain Tissue Resource Center http://www.brainbank.mclean.org/

National Institute of Mental Health: "Teenage Brain: A Work in Progress" http://www.nimh.nih.gov/health/publications/ teenage-brain-a-work-in-progress.shtml

National Sleep Foundation: "Have You Been Sleeping Smart?" http://www. sleepfoundation.org/site/c.huIXKjMoIxF/ b.2417141/k.C6oC/Welcome.htm

Nature Reviews/Neuroscience. "Early Language Acquisition: Cracking the Speech Code" http://ilabs.washington.edu/ kuhl/pdf/Kuhl_2004.pdf

Neuroscience for Kids http://faculty. washington.edu/chudler/neurok.html

PBS: "The Secret Life of the Brain" http://www.pbs.org/wnet/brain/episode1/ infantvision/flash.html

Science News. Org: "Incan Skull Surgery" http://www.sciencenews.org/view/ generic/id/31466/title/Incan_skull_surgery

Trivedi, Bijal P. "Harvard Brain Bank Faces Shortage of 'Normal' Brains." *National Geographic News*, August 28, 2003. http://news.nationalgeographic.com/ news/2003/08/0828_030828_tvbrainbank. html

University of Washington Institute for Learning and Brain Sciences http:// ilabs.washington.edu/about/index.html

Vastag, Brian. "Waking Up: Brain Stimulator Spurs Dramatic Improvement Years After Injury." *Science News*, August 1, 2007. http:// www.sciencenews.org/view/generic/id/8787/ title/Waking_Up_Brain_stimulator_spurs_ dramatic_improvement_years_after_injury

Walker, Amélie. "Neolithic Surgery." *Archaeology*, September/October 1997. http://www.archaeology.org/9709/ newsbriefs/trepanation.html

Further Reading

Clayborne, Anna. *The Usborne Complete Book of the Human Body*. London: Usborne Publishing, 2006.

Newquist, H. P. *The Great Brain Book*. New York: Scholastic Reference, 2005.

Simon, Seymour. *The Brain: Our Nervous System*. New York: HarperCollins, 2006.

Smith, Penny, Sr., ed. *First Human Body Encyclopedia*. New York: DK Publishing, 2005.

Index

Boldface indicates illustrations.

61

About the Author

Kathleen Simpson lives in the hill country of central Texas with her two children, husband, and dogs. She has authored numerous books for young people. In addition to *National Geographic Investigates: The Human Brain,* she has also written *National Geographic Investigates: Extreme Weather* and *National Geographic Investigates: Genetics* for the Society.

Consultant

After attending medical school at the University of Oklahoma, Dr. Lori Jordan completed her training in Pediatrics and Child Neurology at the Johns Hopkins Hospital in Baltimore, Maryland. Her research focuses on children with stroke and brain hemorrhage. Her favorite moments include seeing a child learn to walk and run well again after suffering a stroke, and teaching medical students how to perform a neurological examination on a child. Dr. Jordan conducts research and sees patients at Johns Hopkins Hospital where she is Assistant Professor of Neurology and Pediatrics.

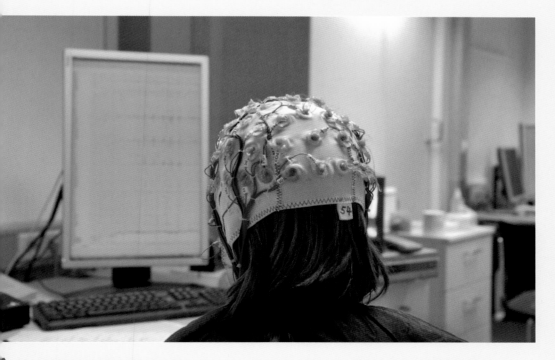

⬆ A net with electrodes is placed on a young woman's head. The computer-generated information about activity in the brain that results will help researchers in their continuing studies of how our brains work.

Founded in 1888, the National Geographic Society is one of the largest nonprofit scientific and educational organizations in the world. It reaches more than 285 million people worldwide each month through its official journal, *National Geographic,* and its four other magazines; the National Geographic Channel; television documentaries; radio programs; films; books; videos and DVDs; maps; and interactive media. National Geographic has funded more than 8,000 scientific research projects and supports an education program combating geographic illiteracy.

For more information, please call 1-800-NGS LINE (647-5463) or write to the following address:

National Geographic Society
1145 17th Street N.W., Washington, D.C.
20036-4688 U.S.A.

Visit us online at
www.nationalgeographic.com/books

For librarians and teachers:
www.ngchildrensbooks.org

More for kids from National Geographic:
kids.nationalgeographic.com

For information about special discounts for bulk purchases, please contact National Geographic Books Special Sales: ngspecsales@ngs.org

For rights or permissions inquiries, please contact National Geographic Books Subsidiary Rights: ngbookrights@ngs.org

Library of Congress Cataloging-in-Publication Data available upon request

Hardcover ISBN: 978-1-4263-0420-0
Library ISBN: 978-1-4263-0421-7

Printed in China

Book design by Dan Banks, Project Design Company

Published by the National Geographic Society

Prepared by the Book Division

Staff for This Book

Manufacturing and Quality Management

Photo Credits

Front cover: An array of electrodes measures brain activity in a Tibetan Buddhist teacher.

Back cover: Various colors highlight the different parts of our complicated human brain.

Page 1: A computer-generated image of the brain's anatomical features

Pages 2–3: Nerve cells in the brain

A Creative Media Applications, Inc. Production